A BILINGUAL BOOK IN ENGLISH AND SPANISH

PIET

WRITTEN BY MARISA BOAN

ILLUSTRATED BY NIKKI CASASSA

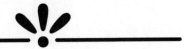

Piet Mondrian is a very famous artist.

Piet Mondrian es un artista muy famoso.

Piet Mondrian was born in Amersfoort in the Netherlands on March 7, 1872. Another name for the Netherlands is Holland.

Piet Mondrian nació en Amersfoort, Países Bajos, el 7 de marzo de 1872. Otro nombre para los Países Bajos es Holanda.

This was near the city of Amsterdam. Amsterdam is known for its historic canals, colorful tulips, and its many bicycles!

Esto estaba cerca de la ciudad de Amsterdam. Ámsterdam es conocida por sus canales históricos, sus coloridos tulipanes y sus numerosas bicicletas.

Bicycles are a very popular mode of transportation in Amsterdam.

Las bicicletas son un modo de transporte muy popular en Amsterdam.

Modes of Transportation

bicycle
la bicicleta

scooter
la patineta

car
el coche
el carro

motorcycle
la motocicleta

train
el tren

bus
el autobús

truck
la comioneta

taxi
el taxi

Modos de transporte

His father and his uncle were both artists. They helped introduce Piet to art. He wanted to be talented like his father and his Uncle Fritz.

Su padre y su tío eran ambos artistas. Ayudaron a introducir a Piet en el arte. Quería tener talento como su padre y su tío Fritz.

In 1892, Mondrian became an art teacher. He was able to work on his paintings while he was a teacher.

En 1892, Mondrian se convirtió en profesor de arte. Pudo trabajar en sus pinturas mientras era profesor.

In the Classroom

teacher
la maestra

desk
el escritorio

chair
la silla

chalkboard
la pizarra

notebook
el cuaderno

pencil
el lápiz

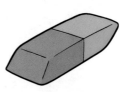

eraser
la goma
de borrar

glue
el pegamento

En el aula

His paintings from this period in his life were of landscapes of the world around him. Landscapes are paintings of nature.

Sus pinturas de este período de su vida eran paisajes del mundo que lo rodeaba. Los paisajes son pinturas de la naturaleza.

He painted scenes from his beautiful country Holland.
The paintings included fields, cows, and windmills.

Pintó escenas de su hermoso país, Holanda. Las pinturas
incluían campos, vacas y molinos de viento.

There are windmills all over Holland!

¡Hay molinos de viento por toda Holanda!

In 1911, he started to paint in a different way. He discovered the style of Cubism from a famous painter named Pablo Picasso. Cubism used shapes to represent things that are real.

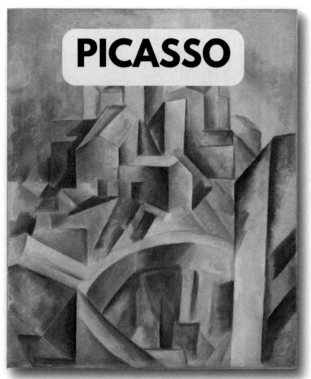

PICASSO

The Reservoir, Horta de Ebro

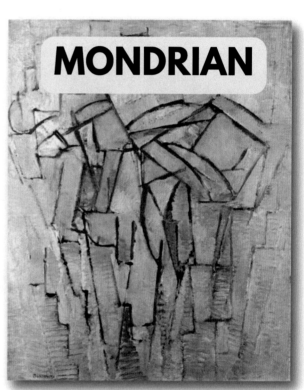

MONDRIAN

Composition in Grey Blue

En 1911 empezó a pintar de una forma diferente. Descubrió el estilo del cubismo de un famoso pintor llamado Pablo Picasso. El cubismo utilizó formas para representar cosas que son reales.

Mondrian started to try this new style of painting and used geometric shapes in his paintings.

Mondrian comenzó a probar este nuevo estilo de pintura y utilizó formas geométricas en sus cuadros.

Geometric Shapes

circle
el circulo

square
el cuadrado

hexagon
el hexágono

triangle
el triángulo

rectangle
el rectángulo

rhombus
el rombo

oval
el óvalo

trapezoid
el trapezoide

Formas geométricas

Mondrian liked the Cubist style, but he wanted to develop his own unique style of painting. He used shapes and lines and called his new abstract style neo-plasticism.

A Mondrian le gustaba el estilo cubista, pero quería desarrollar su propio estilo de pintura. Usó formas y líneas y llamó a su nuevo estilo abstracto neoplasticismo.

He liked to use primary colors, red, blue, and yellow, and lots of straight black lines. He called these simple shapes and designs "basic forms of beauty".

Le gustaba usar colores primarios, rojo, azul y amarillo, y muchas líneas negras rectas. Llamó a estas formas y diseños simples "formas básicas de belleza".

His geometric shape paintings became very famous.
Other painters copied his style over the years.

Sus pinturas de formas geométricas se hicieron muy famosas.
Otros pintores copiaron su estilo a lo largo de los años.

His shapes will live on in new paintings and even in fashion designs of clothing.

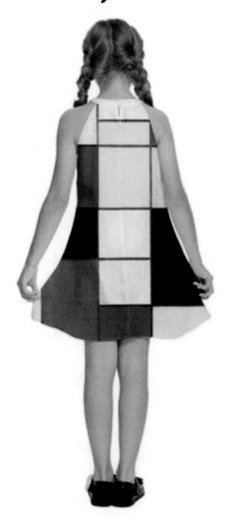

Sus formas perdurarán en nuevas pinturas e incluso en diseños de ropa de moda.

Everyone just loves those simple shapes!

¡A todos les encantan esas formas simples!

Paintings

MONDRIAN SHAPES

PAINTING PROJECT

ART PROJECTS FOR KIDS

Make a Mondrian Masterpiece

Supplies:

- Drawing Paper or poster board
- Painter's Tape
- 3 Different Colors of Paint
- Black and White Paint
- Paint Brush
- Pencil or marker (to draw lines)
- Ruler

Make a Mondrian Masterpiece

STEP 1

Tape off a pattern of squares and rectangles on your page using painter's tape.

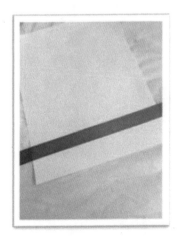  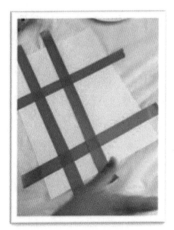

Make a Mondrian Masterpiece

STEP 2

Choose 3 different colors of paint.
Paint the squares and rectangles.
You can paint some spaces in WHITE.
Try not to place the same color in
boxes that are right next to each other.

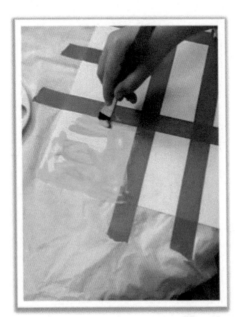 

Make a Mondrian Masterpiece

STEP 3

Carefully remove the tape.
Using a ruler, draw straight lines
around the shapes in black.

Make a Mondrian Masterpiece

STEP 4

Paint the space between the lines using black paint.

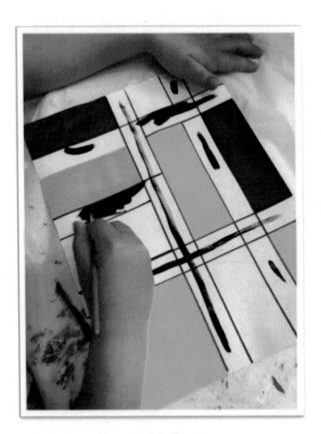

Award Winning
BILINGUAL ART BOOKS

Beautiful bilingual biography books to add to your collection. The easy-to-read text makes these books ideal for young readers. Each book includes a hands-on art project.

LEARN NEW VOCABULARY
English and Spanish

amazon.com

Literacy-based Art Instructional Resources & Books

MAGICSPELLSFORTEACHERS.COM

LITERACY-BASED ART INSTRUCTION

Available at
amazon

Made in the USA
Las Vegas, NV
30 April 2024